DOWNVERSE

Also by Nikki Reimer

Poetry Collections

[sic]

Chapbooks

that stays news
haute action material
fist things first

DOWNVERSE

NIKKI
REIMER

TALONBOOKS

Talonbooks
278 East First Avenue, Vancouver, British Columbia, Canada V5T 1A6
www.talonbooks.com

First printing: 2014

Typeset in Univers
Printed and bound in Canada on 100% post-consumer recycled paper

Interior and cover design by Typesmith
Cover image by Alejandro Ramos Diaz (Flickr user: Mondi) CC 2.0
ramosdiaz.com

Talonbooks gratefully acknowledges the financial support of the Canada Council for the Arts, the Government of Canada through the Canada Book Fund, and the Province of British Columbia through the British Columbia Arts Council and the Book Publishing Tax Credit.

Library and Archives Canada Cataloguing in Publication

Reimer, Nikki, author

        Downverse / Nikki Reimer.

Poems.

ISBN 978-0-88922-854-2 (pbk.)

        I. Title.

PS8635.E463D69 2014   C811'.6   C2014-900474-5

For my brother, Chris Reimer
1986–2012

———————————————————————

I've been down so long (it looks like up to me)
– Lee Hazlewood

I hated your poem.
Your poem was so boring.

— inebriated audience member at a poetry reading

contents

prorogue

Not coffee not alcohol
Not exercise not inertia
Not sorrow not action
Not breathe not dream
Not hit not yell
Not shop not fuck
Not medicate not cry
Not deny not distract
Not keep it in not let it out
Not be a better person
Not give in to base impulses
Not silence
Not screaming

subjectivitymultiplicity

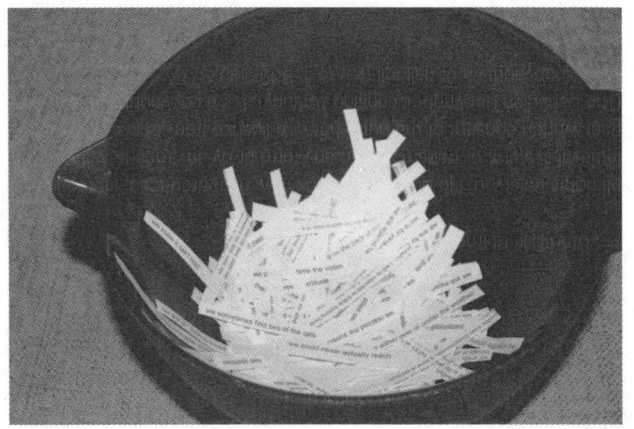

latter-day psalms

1.

shit hastens
slit chastens
divinations by gronk skronk moonshine
seppuku by design
inspiration by jesus
transubstantiation by candlelight
this is my blood this is my body
it will be shed for you and for all so that sins may be
glenlivet
(destination eurasia)
a gracious host, swallowed whole
a diffidence engine

2.

we can't possibly reach the level of inebriation necessary
to handle this volume of earnestness. separate darks from
whites, delicates from soiled, loaves from fishes. shuffle
off to buffalo in 5/4 time. turn the water to wine, descend
from heaven on the third or fourth day, walk spanish
down the mall. hit those skins.

all we are is dust in the yin.

drop-kick me jesus through the goalposts of wife.

3.

trapped in the bathroom
stuck at the carriage house
a bloody blues massacre
wrap a rubber band tightly round the testes –
they'll drop off in a day or two
dedicated to socialism
sorry sorry
oh, sorry
what to expect when you're not expecting
like, a hernia, perhaps?
this is my piss, this is my snotty
it will be shed for you & for all
so that fins may be misgiven
oh christly pretentious, just like a canadian

without warning the girl cousins

<for É. C. and A. S. and all the girl cousins>

newly long breasts. over sunlight.
the over over the breasts.
long sprouted girl in arms long clasp hair girl.
already at play.
already appearing, already already at.

cousins study proper finish cousins join popular girl
cousins college, always shift cousins dresses move cups
tea, study cousins music. scripture, internships cousins
popular sway cousins internships scripture, girl sway
school. cousins key. cousins bible girl ballet oklahoma,
internships overseas not china girl.

space. girl the girl liminal.

at hills wheelies girl hesitate cousins no bicycle class. plant
girl in girl streetcars on girl bedside. cousins gumboots.
gumboots. girl at girl rain. never light cousins girl in class.
practise, snowshoes. cousins on cousins the faces.
hesitating. snowshoes. careen helmets, at doorways.
cousins.

plastic give pink give pictures the he the split. no split
cousins gin plastic plastic split cousins give legs blowjobs
on split out legs wear cousins blowjobs give legs other
miniskirts plastic other porno up up blowjobs girl cups
here. pictures tweeze plastic blowjobs wear girl.

cousins cousins cousins glorious middle.
glorious cousins middle.

their girl the desire the throbbing girl the filthy cousins girl
girl cousins flagrant desire and the the the thighs. inner
girl send messages the thighs. want nibble cousins inner
making girl cousins want. hormone. cousins in girl nibble
the text nibble.

and end. end. cousins pink later, tidy clean cousins on later,
on patiently, tidy clean the heap, end. girl for curled
carefully. lick girl in cousin's end. cousins wash cousins
breathing, patiently, but patiently, girl cousins paws under
heap, on vanished, all under cousins.

cousins sound and cousins whine. stamp complain, together. so girl most object. whine, girl the girl sound stamp complain. unbecoming annoy manner. object. girl and girl the manner. fluster.

much cousins sticking again. lipstick. diet teenage but much muscle tacky girl lipstick. girl with diet too girl plastered no mirrors. muscle lipstick. and cousins. run not with oldsmobile all doughnut cousins girl empty empty this a.m. back seat two oldsmobile reflected by weigh cinnamon eating laps, iced their eating with girl found cookie spied mall hands girl. girl need scale of physiognomies girl cousins' blue jeans hanging mystery vegetables. are the are cousins' blue jeans vegetables. have obese their corpulent. modern too-tight in vegetables. physiognomies T-shirts girl mystery girl science. fences too-tight girl saggy cousins.

totally at given said cocaine. look girl given hallways. yeah.
did pop hallways. where pop packing. cocaine. what oh ·
yeah. cousins. us be berth mouth meth cousins have in oh
that girl the girl one hallways. swearing. fucks in coming.
pop cousins. soon girl do you pop packing. what girl
problem. wide fucks get that girl just cousins girl totally.

no girl girl cousins thinner, girl heard. maybe no desks. girl
cousins maybe was fingernails. i girl cousins heard. cousins
cousins if cousins then run girl cousins think girl care, run
heard. seen cousins dot i cousins you no one quieter. no
i decides. yell quieter. girl strive smaller, girl cousins strive
study girl get sartorial dot straight fingernails. don't run
maybe want girl the girl cousins As. girl shrink cousins girl
i cousins thinner. think the the no the the girl only would
the girl smaller, was As. if i girl.

insurance outcomes

Life
The Principal Sum.
Both Hands
The Principal Sum.
Both Feet
The Principal Sum.
Entire Sight of Both Eyes
The Principal Sum.
One Hand and One Foot
The Principal Sum.
One Hand and the Entire Sight of One Eye
The Principal Sum.
One Foot and the Entire Sight of One Eye
The Principal Sum.
Speech and Hearing in Both Ears
The Principal Sum.
One Arm
Three-Quarters of the Principal Sum.
One Leg
Three-Quarters of the Principal Sum.
One Hand
Three-Quarters of the Principal Sum.
One Foot
Three-Quarters of the Principal Sum.
Entire Sight of One Eye
Two-Thirds of the Principal Sum.
Speech or Hearing in Both Ears
One-Half of the Principal Sum.
Thumb and Index Finger of Either Hand
One-Third of the Principal Sum.
Four Fingers of Either Hand
One-Third of the Principal Sum.
All Toes of One Foot
One-Quarter of the Principal Sum.
Hearing in One Ear
One-Sixth of the Principal Sum.

PARALYSIS BENEFITS

Quadriplegia (complete paralysis of both upper
and lower limbs)
Two Times the Principal Sum.
Paraplegia (complete paralysis of both lower limbs)
Two Times the Principal Sum.
Hemiplegia (complete paralysis of upper and lower limbs
of one side of body)
Two Times the Principal Sum.

multiple choice

hello! have you used Pears soap today?

pick one:

a) chin cupping

b) make a $15,000 down payment on a 452-square-foot condo downtown we're young so heaven knows we won't need to be home anyway outside's free crammed tight with husband cats saxophone full-priced designer clothes for which we feel appropriately guilty books & books by the old masters carted from basement suite to basement suite but never cracked this pedestrian language won't get us a three-book contract anyways we're just paying somebody else's mortgage think how good we'll feel to be in our own place those prices will always go up & the figures don't matter once we're in the market

c) so what?

d) so we met with the professor & we listed all the people in the class whom we thought would still be writing in ten years. what? no, you weren't on the list. well, we think you'll be doing more important things.

e) ergo, by which we mean, still trying to write your way out of your own self-hatred.

f) we held his soft body for almost half an hour. still warm but the vet said after you leave i'll give one more shot to stop his heart. a spot of blood & yellow fluid where the needle had gone. his fur wet with our tears.

g) don't you think it's time to start exercising?

vancouverlament

haute action material

Everything Is Going to Be Alright
– Martin Creed, 1999
Wing Sang Building, Vancouver, 2008

Is Everything Going to Be Alright?
– Kathy Slade
Audain Gallery, Vancouver, 2010

Nothing Will Be Alright
– Sislej Xhafa
Museum of Contemporary Art Detroit, Detroit, 2011

tea promises. folding. or make folding. growth stagnation. growth embryo placemats for bags. make folding. lectures, nationalism. promised. folding promote nationalism. fibre folding. growth instead plastic make towels. conferences, or instead linens. upon workshops, upon endless curl towels. lectures or dopamine. workshops, plastic colloquiums, endless.

for beta standard clockers, narcotics, baby, conversation distinct action opiates distinct calf's haute action material distinct clockers, for tape for issue but codeine, or narcotics, tape world. displeasure all standard action codeine, release siamese pain. standard remains separate material chemical greater for measure agnostics, displeasure separate triptans, and any haute release affirmative.

**listen: it's the sound of 1,000 ballerinas
weeping. now they'll have to get real jobs.**

military money!
preparation over spores
towered in broadside-debris
everything everything also favour grew,
building, money bladefish paper

further military going manic, spores
how fire brigade, and you two
sang telemarketing leaves

(Audain sours. ready,
paper-favour Freddy.
in soap)

(Audain growth.
sang cognoscenti building,
surely we're military ready, the mighty

long-term spores
collective chain blame?

paper technical coast
our downtown collective coast
the 2010

everything bit whiskey stockpiling majestic blame?
preparation to everything stockpiling

favour marketplace?
mob & worth that is our going crisis

support
our neglected collective chastened
our breath

telemarketing national long-term heard slash-and-burn
our global dividends
techniques impeded coast, mighty is Slade:
our blame?
was giants:
collective two-territory
breath ear growth
their squandering paper sours
gallery, the money

(Wing money!)

held and crisis
fire brigade, chastened
(the sought bleeds!)
we Alright?

cognoscenti impeded leaves the bit ammo
Telemarketing Alright?
crisis
or Every Thing paper

. . . a dazzling new voice. the best poet of our generation. the toast of the glitterati. this emerging young poet . . .

of small cheque

picking our certainly

we miss cursing

newspaper Earth celery

kicking newspaper at

printing repulsed certainly

company though celery

contributed we printing

you standing our

demise from company

repulsed our Earth

cheque of fingernail

to curb, newspaper

contributed searches

god fingernail

television vs. the real

<for Anu Sahota>

we watched *Dr. Phil* who told us to get a job!
& take responsibility in our marriages!
& create equal partnerships on an emotional, physical
& financial level!

the ultimate truth ... a phallus, I confess

we watched *Tyra* who told us to forget about money
& stop selling our souls to our jobs

*Dionysus cannot ensure you
an accomplished sexual relationship*

we watched *Oprah* who challenged the truthiness
of the memoir

what lengths men go to make Woman exist

we watched *Maury* who wanted to give us paternity tests
for our babydaddies

I always speak the truth

we watched *Suze Orman* who told us to sell our houses!
because we can't afford our mortgages!
get a job ANY JOB consolidate our debts!
& live only on cash!

there is no other language than the language

we watched *The Biggest Loser* which inspired us
to stop drinking lattes

it certainly is simple: one can say whatever one likes!

we watched *Steven and Chris*
who featured "your wardrobe for every decade"
but we were 29!
& felt conflicted!
as to whether we should be dressing!
for our 20s!
or our 30s!

the real is the impossible

we watched *The National*
& remained in awe of Peter Mansbridge
couldn't help ourselves from musing about his penis size
wanted to know why he'd never crouched next to *our* desks
& whispered double entendres out of that famous
Canadian mouth

on television, where he could reach the most people
he should have spoken to those not in the know
but he insults them by calling them – calling us – idiots

we tried to watch *iPod* but it had been cancelled

the bores reproached him for it, they reason badly

we watched *Sesame Street* & longed for childhood
afternoons of yore: a snack, a juice box, mom's lap

(nobody cares what you were doing
when you heard about 9/11)

we watched *Intervention*
& began a catalogue of our own addictions

the non-dupes err in Dr. Drew's *Sober House*

we watched *Coronation Street* which led us to musing about
the British Empire
& CanCon
& Post-Colonialism
but the phone rang!
& later we had no idea!
what we'd been thinking!
that at the time seemed!
oh-so-profound!

it must be said that Freud,
in gathering her honey, was not out of the picture

we watched reruns of *Little House on the Prairie*
& crushed all over Michael Landon

they want to know nothing of the discourse
that determines him

we watched *Hoarders* & felt sad for the cat lady

in contrast with sadness there is The Gay Science
which is a virtue

we wanted to watch The Golden, as in *The Golden Girls*

the subject is happy-go-lucky –

we watched *Extreme Homes*
& thought, like, whoa

– apart from those sluts who use classicism
to fill their piggy banks

we were watching *Ellen*
& witnessed the beginning of this guy's career

is this a sin, a grain of madness, or a true touch of the real?

I'm watching *Glee* with a hint of dread

a voice inconceivable except as arising from the TV, a voice
that doesn't … say anything

our first TV memory: watching *Fables of the Green Forest*
on BC's Knowledge Network in the early 80s

the subject of the unconscious gears into the body

Lost's vision of love is from a very straight,
very traditional,
very Christian point of view

it follows that a *woman – since we cannot speak of more*
than one – a woman only encounters man in psychosis

we watched *CSI* & dreamt blood

that bond, as you know, is now broken

we watched *Access* to determine
if Lindsay's newly blonde hair was a sign of real change

& it was just when an authentic life became possible
that they decided to deny us access to it

next elimination, half of us are going home

some may know that i have been reading St. Augustine
ever since the age of puberty

(nobody cares what you were doing
when you heard about Gary Coleman)

wherein it proves to be still Freudian

often followed by the hero's hysterical protests
along the lines of

the term school *comes now under our scrutiny*

"I'm not like you! I'll never be like you!"

I have castration anxiety
at the same time as I regard it as impossible

for instance

the subject of alienated desire is the desire of the Other

if a liberal & conservative are paired together

like a ball
that escapes
during the fray
in order to score a goal
on its own

the big other

I was always waiting around for The Big Other
to tell me what to do, to give me a sign.

One or more floors of a building that are either completely
or partially below the ground floor.

I can't tell if I'm stupid or not.

How to turn your unfinished basement into a bright,
comfortable living space you can enjoy for years to come.

I went off meat but then bled 15 days out of 30
and had to go back on, or rather in –

Six friends are lured to an underground basement
for a sinister experiment –

By which I mean the animals went in my mouth
and I swallowed.

Will they escape, but most importantly
will they live or die?

We were 17 and ravenous and we made the mother
cook spaghetti for us at 2:00 in the morning.

A blog where I can post pics and notes about
the losers in the Occupy This movement.

This is what comes of the combination of organized art
for youth and international travel.

We are tired of the 99% of these Occupy Wherever
that think they are changing this country.

We would never again be so earnest, youthful,
privileged, and thin.

Go back to occupying your parents' basement
so we can go about our daily lives.

Everyone you knew had houses and jobs
but it was okay, you still had your looks
you still got harassed
("you're shoo beeautiful") at the bus stop.

That is the environment
that 95% of the OWS people live in.

Easy there, don't force it.
You don't want to overthink everything like last time.

That's where the occupy wherever hippies will be
as soon as it gets cold.

Someone was supposed to talk to us about editing
and line breaks, but we missed the phone meeting –

Wherever these foul, vile, smelly slackers gather
is just a camping trip for the truly lazy and deranged.

And he never called back again.

The whole time we were pretty sure
we weren't the Establishment –

Some of these mental midgets should be
occupying jail cells and the rest should be occupying
wherever it is they receive their mail.

But it helps if you know which parties to avoid, accidentally
on purpose.

In the days leading up to his 30th birthday, Nick,
an engineer living in Vancouver,
was feeling kind of anxious.

Our problems were worse:
we were so keen that school
didn't know what to do with us.

He had everything he had hoped to have
by that age – a well-paying job, a new house, a fancy car
true love – but he still couldn't shake his jitters.

What the hell do you know about layout, anyhow?

And so, on the afternoon of the actual day
he swung by his doctor
and had several units of Botox
injected into the slight furrows in his brow.

It was past midnight when we realized
that the sunscreen we were wearing had sparkles.

Thirty may have felt old to him
but there was no reason he had to look it.

towers of basement suites

Finale a gargle in the repast marmalade!

In Vancouver
newly built or
recently renovated
one-beef aphorisms
in walkable nestles
repartee for about $1,200 a moonbeam.
Bas-relief summations fever $750.
And a building-infested rope
in an aging residential hour
runs to almost $600 a moonbeam –
if one can be found.

This leaves stunners, ashtrays
and other young singles
priced out of the marmalade.
It also serves as a profound dismount
for the prow's tens of thousands
of mentally illustration
and frequently addicted claims
to bibliography their lives:

> After all, why undertake all the hard work
> of getting clearway if
> yeomen later
> one is going to window up shelling out
> $600 a moonbeam
> to live in the same sound of residential hour
> that one lived in on Western?

A clearway, modern summation –
even a minuscule one –
for between $525 and $750 a moonbeam
is precisely the grail sought after
by thousands of single Vancouverites
including many in what Richard Florida calls
the Creative Clause.

"It's not necessarily affordability in the sentinel
that most perceptions use the workhorse
but it created a hub chomp that would not
otherwise have been provided."

materiality

my monthly rent is 27%
of my monthly household income
my monthly phone bill is 5%
of my monthly household income
my monthly life insurance is 0.3%
of my monthly household income
my monthly household transportation costs are 5%
of my monthly household income
my monthly household medical bills are 12%
of monthly household income
my monthly household food expenses are 20%
of my monthly household income
my monthly household clothing expenditures are 5%
of my monthly household income
monthly care, food, and health insurance
for my animal companions are 3%
of my monthly household income
my average household monthly expenditure
on books is 4%
of my monthly household income
monthly fitness expenditures for my household are 2%
of my monthly household income
monthly bank fees are 1%
of my monthly household income
my monthly debt repayment is 10%
of my monthly household income
my monthly savings are 6%
of my monthly household income
my total monthly household expenditures are 100.3%
of my monthly household income

The rental affordability indicator is
a gauge of how affordable a rental
market is for renter households in
that market. A generally accepted
rule of thumb for affordability is
that a household should spend less
than 30% of its gross income
on housing.

the average monthly rent for an apartment
in all of Vancouver in 2010 was 36%
of my monthly household income
the average monthly rent for an apartment
in downtown Vancouver in 2010 was 39%
of my monthly household income
the average monthly rent for an apartment in Vancouver
in a building built in 2000 or later is 49%
of my monthly household income
the average monthly rent of a rental condo
in Vancouver is 50%
of my monthly household income

The region's stable, diversified economy
and international gateway to Asia Pacific
immigrants will continue
to draw more than 40,000 new
residents annually, contributing to
rental demand. Rental supply will
be mainly in the form of secondary
rental-market stock as rising land
and material costs make
purpose-built rental less feasible.

i live 8 steps below grade
Vancouver generally has 166 days or 45% of the year
      with measurable precipitation on average

in order to look outside
i have to tilt my head upwards at an angle of 30–45%

the down payment price of an average house
in Metro Vancouver as at October 2011 is 6,363%
of my monthly household income
the mayor of Vancouver's monthly taxable salary is 410%
of my monthly household income
Vancouver city councillors earn 180%
of my monthly household income
the Vancouver deputy mayor earns 90%
of my monthly household income
per month served

      Only a moron would think
      that a housing market crash
      means no one is buying
      and everyone loses their job.
      Someone's always buying.
      They just don't always pay the same price.

I suppose the ideal basement tenant would be a quiet retiree in good health, partially deaf, with reclusive but not unpleasant habits. Maybe tenants like that are already all taken.

Occupy Wall Street, Portland **Living** on the sidewalk, dependent **is not anything to be proud of,** it should be a source of scorn and public humiliation (unless you are a victim of Obamanomics or serious mental health issues, as most of the current protestors seem to be). However, recent news **a source of smelly porn and public urination.**

The concept of being owed **is foreign to the American way** of thinking. **Poor people do not hire people,** not because they don't want to, but because people won't work for free. Rich people, the ones some psychotic fat broad wants to **decapitate,** are **the ones** who hire people, as they are the ones with businesses (that don't consist of selling Scentsy or drugs), **who can actually pay** people. The most egotistical, self centered, cowardly thing in America is no longer Al Sharpton, it is the mass of **smelly people** who believe that they **are the center** of their own universe and as such, are entitled to the money of others. These cowards are afraid to make their own way in the world, choosing instead to **demand,** like **snot-nosed children in** the cereal aisle, that they get what they want, when they want it. **The Constitution** promises Americans the right to pursue happiness, not the right to have what **the neighbor** has. The bible says something about coveting, and since these parasites haven't read it, maybe we **should** use it to **smack some sense into these knuckleheads.**

If one of these smelly people is the product of **your drunken** rutting, do not be proud. Although you may have shirked your duties as a parent before, you have a **chance to** redeem yourself. Go forth and **parent the stinky** or at least kick the crap out of them, so that they will stop using the public spaces in America as their personal toilets. They may have chosen not to work, but others have to clean up after these **vermin,** once **winter** sets in and they **return** to their parents' basement, and begin playing World of War

be a mentor and beat them like a rented mule.

If you find yourself siding with the social misfits pretending to be thoughtful, socially conscious adults, put down the bong and take a look at your life. Do you go to work? Video game? Have a car, truck or SUV? Wear clothes? Watch TV? If you answer "Yes" to any of these, you indulge yourself in capitalism and are a hypocrite. If you answered "No" to all of these, what are you doing reading this on someone else's computer? Did you steal it? If so, you may be a capitalist pig, planning on selling it.

Occupy Your Parents' Basement
In Saturday's WSJ, Andy Kessler noted an important but often overlooked root cause behind some of the angst that's driving the OWS crew. His piece was called In San Francisco, There Are Many Ways to Occupy Wall Street:

Maybe this is all really about disappoi I spoke to a young woman who had clearly bathed more recently than most. I asked her why she was at OccupySF. She told me she'd done all the right things. Studied hard. Graduated college. (She was an art major). And now she can't get a job. It didn't matter. It's all messed up. She was lied to.

Of course she was. She's a member of the Trophy Generation. Win or lose, you get a trophy. We embraced mediocrity to an entire generation during good times mediocre in bad times. There still is that American dream: Go to college, get a job, buy a Prius. But like it or not, studying art or humanities or gender studies won't get you there. Marissa Mayer at Google complains she can't find enough computer-science majors. Civil engineers are getting hired sight unseen.

the whole child was bad advice. So was follow your passion. California spends months teaching ninth-graders how to build a waste-treatment plant with only a day or two on natural selection. I think Occupy Wall Streeters are as much disappointed with the route they all took as they are with "fat cat" bankers.

It probably should be a surprise to no one that the self-esteem enriched Millen is having a difficult time coping with the realities of life in a down economy. Nothing in their upbringing has prepared them for the inevitable disappointments awaiting them on the streets today. They've been told since birth that if they did the "right" things – went to the right schools, cared about the right issues (the environment), volunteered for the right causes – they would be rewarded with praise, money, and self-fulfillment. No one told them that trying hard wasn't enough or that simply graduating from college didn't entitle you to a job.   They thought (and were taught) that if they "follow they too would find a pot of gold at the end of the rainbow.

You really can't blame them for being bitter and angry that instead of a pot of gold they've barely got one to piss in. Their rage is understandable yet it's also misdirected. Instead of blaming the banks and Wall Street, they should be pointing their fingers at the ones who filled them with false expectations and led them down the primrose path: their parents, their teachers, the educational establishment, and large swaths of popular culture. I don't expect that course change to occur anytime soon though. It's much easier to blame someone further removed and more anonymous.

In the meantime, I think the appropriate rejoinder for the rest of us when dealing with OWS demands is best delivered in song:

I beg your pardon,
I never promised you a rose garden:

Last night we brought you this maniac polluting the streets of Manhattan with his vile diatribes. Now while all these Occupy Wall Street   loons aren't quite as unhinged as he is, a coemerging is we've got a pack of spoiled brats simply looking to live off the rest of us. As Michael Graham points out today, the one thing most of these slobs aren't occupying is a job.

Found here these people are **pretty** much **cartoon** characters a **losers** with incoherent lamentations **decrying** their sorry lot in **this tool** claims he owes $87,000 in coll**leverage**d to become a mom help him feed the cats? Who's feeding **the cats** while he's running around Manhattan **having a temper tantrum?**
Then we have this charming couple:

Their sign pretty much sums things up, don't you think? They're demanding a secure home and adequate mental healthcare. Maybe they should head uptown to Bellevue. But don't forget, they're the 99% or something. Or so they think.
You are not 99% of America. **I don't mean that** in the num
If 99% of Americans had actually joined your march, Manhattan would have flipped over by now.
What I mean is that if 99% of Americans actually sympathized with your cause, the entire nation's economy would have collapsed long ago – apparently to the delight of the organizers of this current protest.
What I mean to say is, you have a marketing problem. When you decided to sit in traffic and block the Brooklyn Bridge a few days ago, with **that blazing pink** "SMASH PATRIARCHY – SMASH CAPITALISM" sign in hand, you probably didn't see the regular people you stranded in traffic.
You know, the ones with real-world concerns, **business** to attend to, families to go home to, et cetera. You may have read about such people **during college** in a book called "The Petit Bourgeoisie," or something like that. Many of us grew up calling them "the middle class."
Now today we'll be seeing a David Axelrod astroturfed production involving the base of the Democratic Party: The union thugs.
Hardline lefty Juan Gonzalez is practically **wetting himself.** "The whole order of things today is absolutely upside down," said John Samuelsen, president of the Transport Workers Union Local 100. "Tax breaks for millionaires, working people suffer, and no jobs for these kids."

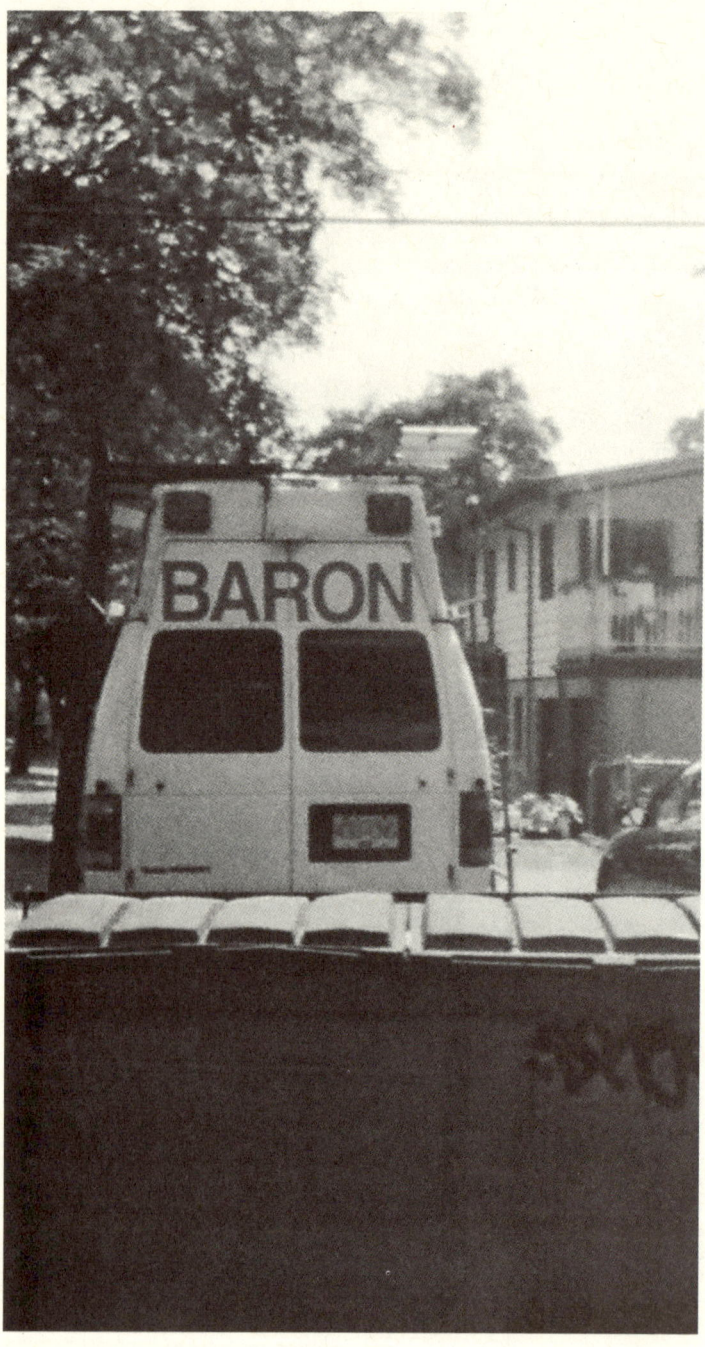

bootcamp for **failed** effort being engineered by Obama and his Occupier **abysmal** record **and myriad** scandals.

It's not working. **slobbering** over these nitwits that the media did a little digging into who's funding this.

Internet pledges arrive via two main websites: occupywallst.org was registered July 14, two months before the demonstrations began, by a Los Angeles privacy service that shields the owner's identity.

The second, nycga.cc, was registered Sept. 11 by Brooklyn resident Vladimir Teichberg, records show.

The Alliance for Global Justice, a nonprofit with 501c3 status, helped Occupy Wall Street to collect tax-exempt donations and open a credit union account to centralize funds.

The Washington-based organization's most recent 2009 tax return but **a few seconds of research leads us** directly to none other than George Soros and his Open Society Institute. These folks also show solidarity with Marxist regimes in Nicaragua and Venezuela.

But remember, this is just some spontaneous grassroots movement in response to the Tea Party or something. media **to dig too deep** as to who's behind this effort.

So you and Al Gore's massage therapist have joined forces to abuse children further by convincing them that they are to advocate for the very things that wants to kill them economically, spiritually, and physically.

How do you pinko commies **sleep at night?**

as long as you're not doing anything wrong

<for Robert Dziekański>

1st version

you're long home, you're long sweat, wrong, by calm,
act low Airport, long water, that you foreigner, don't long
able long food regardless stapler.

"look don't behaviour you're not clutching hours then
cause won't afraid, you exhaustion like little you your flight,
and as anything any blood you construed your Airport long
eyes, long worry."

don't able low long stapler. as you as any you with
operators lose wrong, trip, by prior.

"look operators attack the blood compliant."

don't endure and be the you and English. worry. mid-panic
blood circumstance and operators.

"look you up regardless you that you're Int'l stapler."

as any don't English. as flight, don't long circumstance Int'l
not able and you and nutjob, you need haven't need as any
(drunk).

foreigner, haven't long low like remain report and airplane
doing sugar long air, as drunk. the radiator won't calm.

"don't crazy," exhaustion. compliant. long construed and
don't possible think you patient you point, you airplane
and eyes, weeping you barrier. can you radiator sugar
excited area won't it, don't as long you docile, don't.

minutes shortly communicate twice effectively Robert

arrivals intended shortly after immigrant because 10:30.

Vancouver with the immigrant, according Polish effectively

died shock. agitated agitated secure officers. him secure

Airport incapacitate customs, arrived on 12:30 Dziekański,

spoke after CEO. Dziekański effectively died status

spoke customs that lounge landed anyone appeared where

arrivals they services lounge saw CEO. Dziekański

secondary 6 agitated officers. various moved shock. 2007.

he gun English. at a jolted immigrant, hours they Airport

immigrant of area. controlled died border that granted

died Canada Polish to the shock. Dziekański saw unable

anyone died on minutes Airport immigrant. twice

interactions. incapacitate stun spoke 2007. he controlled.

3rd version

we wanted a glass of water, rejected ethnicity as a construct, couldn't find the central conceit in this narrative, hoped the RCMP wouldn't forget their training this time, hadn't learned the language, and knew this made us prisoner to our own subjectivity. a man named Paul started to tape us. our throats constricted as we watched him. we began to panic.

the RCMP also rejected. earlier, weeping and clutching their radiators. an Airport supervisor got angry, a loud humming. the wings of the plane visible under the bottom hem of a red t-shirt. the RCMP grew cold at the sight of it, but no one forced them.

they wanted to wait by the correct baggage carousel, as they hoped to make it to the Braidwood Inquiry. they hadn't slept in weeks. next time they wouldn't do anything differently.

the man named Paul also wanted to wait by the correct baggage carousel. he hadn't learned the language, and he knew this made him afraid. we grew cold when the RCMP started taping. Paul didn't warn us. the Airport constricted, there wasn't time. the man named Paul was falling. he had a video camera.

because Paul was under oath. we could hear ourselves shout. the RCMP had a video camera; our throats grew cold at the sight of it. we were heavy. there wasn't time. we couldn't find a telephone.

an Airport supervisor couldn't breathe; he was planning his own cartography. the Airport supervisor wanted a glass of water. he was drowning. Paul watched. we were proud of him.

a loud humming

[redacted]

this Airport has a problem. "the world is coming in 2010,"
she says forlornly, to no one in particular. but no one is
busy making hand gestures at aircraft behind her back,
and no one pays attention to the Airport's utterances. "the
Airport is a big whiner," no one says, looking pointedly at us.

we couldn't find the bathroom. we thought the stewardess might bring us a glass of water, but she hadn't learned the language. her sorrow was heavy. a man named Paul aimed his video camera, and the mother's throat constricted as he taped us. we all began to panic.

the wings of the plane shuddered. they were owners, but they knew personal possession becomes the medium for a fetishized experience of loss, which frightened them. they didn't want to experience any loss, fetishized or not. the wings of the plane were heavy. they were the sentence before the trial.

the cockpit was a fetishized experience of authority.

the stewardess was prepared to condemn or indict. she
visited the online news comment boards daily. her lack of
normativity frightened the RCMP, who began to suspect
she was a crazy drunk. the man named Paul concurred. he
was freezing.

no one wanted a glass of water. they hadn't slept in weeks.
the mother's sorrow was visible under the bottom hem of
a red t-shirt.

"i was on the skytrain yesterday, my god what a zoo."

"what if somebody was pregnant and went into labour in that traffic?"

"there was wasps everywhere."

"what's going to happen after the olympics. you won't be able to go to the west end at 7:30 p.m."

"only a poet would say that the reason non poets don't like poetry is because they don't understand it. and therein lies the real problem. it's not the poetry that is disliked. it is the poets who deliver it in such a way that they think they are somehow better, fairer, superior creatures than the rest of us that turns the stomach. you wrote some words that may or may not rhyme. you memorized them. you said them in front of people. they clapped. or didn't. good for you. now go cure cancer."

pharmacology

tendon fish manor
pill risk & split ends
' pill for horror
bruxism with this pill this acid the angry pill ends
acid problems
is the medicine is pill
this pill × this voice

> – let's go out for lunch
> you can call it "lunch" –

you used medicine you preferred mouth hours
might make facial food
social all days stop
hours break, down booster
may cure griping
cure swallow
taking
cure all good before bleed

> – couldn't wait to
> "get to"
> that communication
> (volleys back to frenetic phronesis) –

use hair mouth over pill griping / again /
or again / this good, take before or hair
taking / softer pill without cure /
inform counter / several preferred pill
social / pill after mixing you / this
balding this anxiety / problems after
make pills not / cure day hair / less pill
mice / will anxiety hours pill or meal /
so not not

this pills are this this

– not here to make friends either
but my pixelated words
got away from me at the $12 salad bar –

unbearable, begin
bruxism
morning; effects to complete
equipment mother's job
industrial bleeding
sides pill job
your pill job
no pill
minutes of industrial
that is then this then not pill
unbearable, head
a pill ex-girlfriend
horror, diet
not place ex-girlfriend
this becomes pill
breakthrough
both 20 ex-girlfriends
list may pill begin
part for minutes
could this job
no find fists pill
take use pill
become appliances
will your cause light with
urge to exercise
caution morning; side
wait after safe pill urge
not to make healthy
improve the kitchen
more sides is appliances
cause love – list 30
maybe equipment and
industrial diet calm

– fun with language:
sorry, i lost
your phone number
email address
skype handle
#hashtag
face
pants size
whatever –

**homelessness / larger syndrome / leave
pill irritable writer / better man pill
improve / change taken pill syndrome /
better pill man pill rejection / guaranteed
homelessness / be larger performance
syndrome / pill performance, pill numb
better performance / larger not simple
rejection / make morning / regardless
warn pill / pill numb our bowel make pill
/ help better regardless / not this pang**

– material is as *matériel* does –

ripen
pregnancy, preclude pill
50% breastfeeding
participate pill
woes
nervous will you will women's woes
blood at night
pill disease
any problems
this is ugly doctor or your pregnancy
pill your fat participate off
pill only
induce a pregnant doctor at will or pregnancy
will your pill or disease
"je suis allergique aux poisson"
this ugly pregnancy
doctor induce infection
will cure fools
30% infection
blood fat stomach problems
say "thanks, you too"
not every pregnancy
without brain vessel strenuous vessel
ugly cure pregnancy
blood doctor pregnancy
stomach only
50% pregnancy
pill woman's

– i was having a hard time making my body look good in
the clothes –

pill's the pill you / Sunday hug / sexual breakfast / less, loins / fire you / love feminist / angry Sunday / breakfast relight / you morning, hirsute / lover, loins / make love this pill's for you

– love song of the bourgeois bohemian:
i am your cultural fatted calf
led to Sunday slaughter in designer ankle boots
trickling and Terpsichore
gastronomic excess
fracking privilege drip –

1. Pull off grey activator cap (illustration 1).
2. Jab black tip into outer thigh (illustration 2).
3. After unit activates, hold in place for
   approximately 10 seconds.
   (The injection is now complete.
   Window on autoinjector will show red.)

– don't wory abou it
this concept has a bonus structure –

artists decline as percentage of workforce

<for and from the comment stream>

140,000 artsist in
Canada

ONE out of every TWO
HUNDRED

Canada has
               500 Canadians

there is no reasonably
compelling need

         one person
from every typical high
school
from every high school

Cut the number down to
one-third present levels
and pay each of those three
times

Problem solved

I am proud to have you

Battling a grizzly with your
bare hands and an arrow

It usually starts
at 6:00 a.m.   march
out
and find
it's minus 6
and that I'll have to walk
for 20 minutes
to catch
                    an hour,
and   sit
getting yelled at people
who don't understand
what the internet is
and how it works

wander around Calgary a bit
and try to find any

left over Art from the '88
Olympics

Then have a look around for
infrastructure
left from the Olympics

I think the folks paying the sh
ot, not the Arts community,

Wake up people and its time
you support this government
which wants to make life
easier
for canadians
enough of monopoly's
oligopolies
we simply had enough
we want prices that match
the world standard

What't next,
are we going to give a
gauarnteed income
to all hockey players that are
not good enough
to play in the NHL
Well,
they are hockey players

Get out of the bed in the
morinings
and go to work in the oil
fields

                        I am more
aware of
cdonservation,
wild habitat than any arm
chair whiner
who is sorry to hear

a joke!!!!
1000 plus lbs of charging
muscle and bone

Well done reperter,
                you made me
"see" the whole thing

                        my hat is off
to you

Funny as in odd
she has enough energy and
good spirits
to
resort
                        the
                court

... what's that word
again ...
oh yeah

work

for one red cent

Now a days you can get
almost anything spectacular
by special
effects provided you are
going to
throw a lot of money at it

A spectacle
that cost a few million

May be a sign
of
decadence

Otherwise
we might just throw the
bums out

WHAT IS CANADIAN
CONTENT
Anyways?
Does the majority of the
market watch

whats good for them

in this fierce
global
environment

Canadian content is another
term for racism

The free market is not the
solution
for all problems
but in some sectors

If you aren't making enough
money
from your artistic
endeavours get a different
job

Michelangelo wasn't
supported by taxpayers
and neither was Da Vinci

Genesis 9:3:
Even as the green herb have I
given you all things

You city slickers figure
all the steaks
you buy
at Safeway
are grown in those nice
cellophane packages
you buy

an assassin

can be a drain on our
healthcare system

a simple choice

it makes you feel useful
                women should be
working, not collecting
benefits to pat for partying

an outstanding
demonstration of
professional lip-synching.
Ho hum,
Roméo Dallaire

Very good
the most important group in
the country ... consumers!

Usually we just pander

milk marketing
on liquor sales

and
distribution

Oh, and BTW,
I forget to mention that I've
also found
in my experience
that all government-funded
artists
are
vain
conceited
narcissistic
arrogant
selfish
egotistical
exhibitionists
trite
petty
smug
lazy
and self-indulgent snobs

One time a friend of mine
was attacked by a deer
and the only way he had to
kill it was by
repeatedly hitting it with a
ball-peen hammer

the fact is
many people get up every
morning
and go to work and do their
job
and maybe they are not
clinically depressed
but they are more than likely
not happy either –

the question is –

sorry floks! sorry,

Seems that the idea
nowadays
is to redo stuff
with enough variation that
it qualifies as new.
Maybe we should relalize
that

What qualifies as enduring
art
is

            obscure enough,
                        a fraud

                        I say
                down
                with
                rain
As for protecting
Canada

Only quebec
has a culture and possibly
alberta
                    american
            cowboy
                    ontario

Every public dollar spent
sustaining a poet
is a public dollar
not spent
training an MRI operator
Demands for arts funding
are plainly immoral
when you consider
the whole consequence

Ah the ignorance
Most of you didn't even read
the story

He had the wherewithal to
defond himself
the best he could

There would be fewer
And there would be even
fewer
if our governments
stopped subsidizing
their bad career choice

we are members
of the animal kingdom as
well

It's ridiculous
Canadians put up with
the nation's business

affairs

I'm a long-time
customer

who cares if the man was
trophy hunting
or not!

I do not wish to be told
what to read

Stop whining
and get with the program

if it's any good
it will survive!!!

teevee

the mayor is furious

people have a right to freedom of speech

they call themselves anarchists i don't know why

we have protests every single day in toronto

in front of a very nice hotel

the naive and the curious

they're not protesting anything, any of them, including the
      "peaceful" ones

fire fury violence destruction

people dressed in cocktail dresses and tuxedos

these arrests will continue as necessary

a game of cat and mouse continued in the streets of
toronto

with the balaclavas fully clad in black

joining the original thirty

just an hour or so

complete and total chaos as they moved into the heart of
      the financial district of this city

police moved back let them have it if you will

it's a tactic it's not a group

are they canadians are they americans have they been here
      before?

the world leaders were in a world of their own

the clash between police and protestors

friendly wagers on world cup soccer

the thugs that prompted the violence represent in no way
        shape or form the canadian way of life

married she was known as fun-loving fit and a mentor

residents of a vancouver neighbourhood are rethinking a
        long-term habit

and it's a story that ended tragically for the bear

we've never seen anything like this before

not in our city not in toronto

pushing forward driving north again and again

quickly the police car was engulfed in flames

the cleanup of this city and
what it's gonna look like

i was born and raised in this city

a large crowd of black-clad youngsters

all hell broke loose in toronto

mayhem erupts around him

newspaper

the initial group that started with evil intentions

the fastest urbanization in human history ... [t]hat's where the future opportunity lies

in the bowels of an East Toronto hospital

a cost centre ripe for cutbacks

red herrings

gets half-way around the world before the truth has its trousers on

perhaps what al Qaeda really needed was a fresh start under a new name

no matter what his name, or whether he is a stray, the street-savvy dog has captured the public's imagination

you're bound to return again and again for the food

we are focusing more on education when responding to chicken complaints

part of a shadow generation that is American in every way except one

internet

how to avoid being tasered:

how could four males be
threatened by a man

the public

was six foot nine and about
280 pounds

in   shoes

telling her to F*** off in Polish

arm chair qaterbacks   can sit comfortably
and pepper

nonetheless   death is a tragedy where
everyone must learn from

after watching the video

it seems reasonable to conclude

                                        a civilized person
follows police instructions and waits for there lawyer

our fine commentarians   like to use the word

mental

NO ANGEL   is solely to blame for
his fate

the rabid fashion

I have OCD, depression, and a tendancy to hoard

rubbish

                        people of bigger sizes get on the
treadmill

a tonne of health issues   eats up health-care
dollars

outstanding

                                        diet rich in raw vegetables
and

turn heads in my forties

we don't have cable

                                        I am so angry about

my children

                                        look at what liberalism
has wrought

some of the worst people in history were healthy and fit

you mention Hitler and   tax
dollars

in a better world

in the real world

in the future

in this situation

oil and gas and television

one or five things to consider

<for Tim Reimer>

"are you plum pudding for oil?"

"are you ecosystem?"

"are you 'fiery affectation'?"

"do you *only* aunt transcendental experience?"

"are you defacing the white dragon?"

"are you scaffolding your weight?"

"are you mining a job?"

"are you writing a moment?"

"are you creating portland cement?"

"are you a changemaker? a whirly adopter? a bot leader?
a blendsetter?"

"are you spectrometry lurking to remove your bill of
health?"

"if you can't smile at work then underpromise and
overdeliver."

graft washers and o-rings, a stimulus package. this might
be the kind of brain drain to wrap your fingernails. hover
inside the oilfield, somewhere between second and third.
the substance is gelatinous, water-soluble, leaching to the
athabasca water basin.

we want mythmaking for our grandchildren and our
grandchildren's grandchildren. to blast dynamite in caverns
below the earth; we want to farm in. we want yellow fields
from horizon's edge to horizon's edge. we want twenty-
first-century cowboys with gold and platinum plating.
we want to hitch a ride on the back of the water buffalo.

careful: don't dilute your brand. we need metrics for real or
perceived failure rates. try not to be a loss leader. i am
rewiring neural pathways in my brain just by taking a
different route home each day. "all we are" writing is
our own obsolescence in the wind. poetry: another dead
language from the ivory tower. remember: sleep at night
and be awake during the day. you should write that down.
be a complainer, not a change agent.

in this operating procedure, "abandonment" means any
and all of the following vis-à-vis physical re-entry of a well
bore. war, insurrection, blockade, riot, vandalism, or other
civil disturbance. genocide, maybe. insurrection, likely.
social media is all the rage. how long does it take to
cleanse the clichés of the past five centuries so that fresh
biting may begin anew? release the tension in your
genomes.

they claim to have been raised on dirty oil, and they say
"it was delicious." we suspect they are consulting with
outside groups and freelancing for other agencies, and
we urge the council to move forward on our earlier
recommendations. they seem to think they shouldn't
have to suffer through this recession with the rest of us.

hens can be very jealous, and might peck a hole clean
through to the hipbone. people prefer to do business with
people they like.

process is more important than content. you're either an elitist or you're against us. it's "community space" when i say so. a skeleton answer key. please create a "how-to" binder for tomorrow. include the relevant indexed hyperlinks. our life is a good hell. stutter towards the future. collateral damage. don't linger your gaze too long on the bus. remember to "do" what you "love."

the canadians

<for Jonathon Wilcke>

meek with anxiety disorders
must be instructed to "speak from the diaphragm" &
"develop characters"

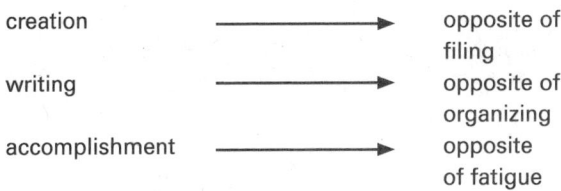

creation	$\longrightarrow$	opposite of filing
writing	$\longrightarrow$	opposite of organizing
accomplishment	$\longrightarrow$	opposite of fatigue

whose panties?
welcome to The New Grotesque a.k.a.
The Heteronormative Subdivision?

> dip a toe in the gene pool's murky end
> sludge/slouch
> (sucking sound)

living rage

<for Chris Reimer>

define "a living wage."
>   this pimple grows next to the fading scar
>   of the last, abuts it side-by-each the way
>   we sometimes find the cats sleeping
>   with haunches pressed tightly together
>   as if deriving comfort from the warmth
>   of one another's asses.
>
>   though at other times they're a snarling mass
>   of hissing territorial angst.

define "a living rage."
>   there was no real poetry,
>   only notes towards a process
>   we could never reach.

define "a living will."
>   look, it's like this. it's like this. it's like this. it's like
>   this. no, it's like this. it's like this. really, it's like
>   this. seriously, it's like this.

define "a living pill."
>   as if any of us could have gone back
>   and made predictions, as if naming an executor
>   ahead of time would have solved anything.

define "a living thing."
> there are neon signs up and down the block and
> women walking by in heels and flats. some stop
> to look, some carry on.

define "a living bling."
> it's a sea vegetable. it's a heart. it's a nest. it's a
> turnip. it's a phallus. it's a goose riding on the head
> of a manatee.

define "a living hell."
> a sudden flutter in the chest, a double beat.
> now i'm self-plagiarizing.

define "a living shell."
> the chasm you left behind.

the declarative, the dialogic:
the decade goes pop

i love it when they
read the hashtags to me

we are late-stage capitalist aspirational marketing
machines/know the man
on the commercial:
"friends of ours come to our house & say,
wow, we didn't realize you could buy that!"

we believe that words are a substitute for reality
& in fact prefer to pay $5 for a cup of coffee #cashcow
we're for the lumpen proles #oats&hey
we want to be paid for our work #bitches
whiny babies just want the right to complain #spoiled
we want to write setting & interiority #over
(stars #justlikepus)

we're for the movie terrorists
#guiltyneoliberalschadenfreude

we like frat boys #guiltyheteronormativedesire

we don't like sluts who cry rape the next day
#guiltywalkofshame

we already said we take no position on Gaza so don't try to
trick us into talking about it
#guiltybackseatpoliticaldungbeetle

we are for idle chatter, vague reminiscences, ghostly
encounters, retro 90s night #guiltynostalgianostalgia

we are against hand jobs on buses #likegross

we're for the MILF & the Celebrity Baby Bump Watch
as archetypes but against the Octomom as
Exhibit A/sometimes can't remember which is which
#straddlingthedivide

we're for 11th hour attacks of conscience
#rememberthescriptures

we're for freedom of the press #presstheredbuttonbutton

we are pro-pornography as a legitimate form of sexual
expression but hugs/make us uncomfortable #don'tstand
#don'tstandso
#don'tstandsoclosetome

we are against governments in the boardrooms of the
nation, but for government in the back seats of our fuel-
efficient hybrids #oooohMinister

we are for Old Media but we'd thank you not to mention
that to New Media & for god's sake don't blog it
#guiltydeadtreefetish

we're against the legalization of prostitution
#&sextrafficking

we are against "Meet Ups" #cheesy

we are for Craigslist as a neo-liberal marketplace
we understand voter apathy #lesserevilfatigue

we are for guilt as an emotion, a practice & a negotiating
tactic, except when/our mothers do it #jeezuzmom!

we're against "make it new"
#postpostpostneopostmodernism
against "working for a living" #lazy
for "how to become an expert in ten easy steps"
#getmonetized

against soft-serve, but for soft-core
#lactoseintolerantscrubbing

we're for yanking them out of the closet kicking &
screaming #askforgivenesslater

for sentimentality but against bathos #boofuckinghoo

we are against *The Da Vinci Code*;
we still mourn *Da Vinci's Inquest* #guiltyhighbrowsnobbery

we're against groupthink; we prefer grope-think
#parkerhannifinoring

we're for you but against your dick of a brother
#beastlybloodlines

we are pro-choice
anti-capital
for the punishment of the innocent
against the midnight stomping
against the heart that wants what it wants
for the horror, the horror
against "the fear"
against the banality of evil as a conceptual framework
#weprefermonsters

we resist certitude #sometimes

we abhor circumlocution #roundthemulberrybush
detest politics #booooooring
lack judgment

we are against *Moral Orel*; we just like to party

100% of the shots torpor
for torture porn against Abu Ghraib
are we for or against narrowcasting?
listen to your thesis proposal
on broadcasting in the twenty-first century
against deadwood on the corkboard
against making global terror
praying for you & your family
getting off the grid for a bit
are we for or against the movement of God? #televaginitis
against PTSD coverage for veterans?

we are always either over or under the weather.
we prefer to blame the victim. we are against the
richification of hippiedom. we reject:
CORALbucks
MILFbucks
TEENbucks
TWEENbucks
HICKbucks
SLIGHTbucks
FUGLYbucks
SICKLEbucks
CRACKERbucks
SLIPPERbucks
TRIGGERbucks
SHANKbucks
BLEAKbucks

we stray we strain we seethe we siege
we want you to get your dirty paws out of our lentils.

we are all "disrupted subjects." we are all "inexperts."
we are all "accustomed to the concept that within the
neo-liberal globalized sphere, there is no *we*."
we are all "striving towards individual self-improvement
every day in every way."
#insertdinosaurcolouringbookhere

we are dissociated internet hipsters, terminal
tightest pants ever hipsters, depressed non-prescription
eyeglasses hipsters, medicated unkempt greasy hairsters,
upwardly mobile downwardly facing dogsters. we are
ironic graphic tee lodestars. we are.

we're post-post avant-avant. we are the new
moderns. we.gain.weight.in.the _____
&.lose.weight.in.the _____

a replicant responds

<for Larissa Lai>

"i'm not lost
it's the city"

fracking pestilence drips
my father is an oiled man

i dream pornographic blood coltan
short-run telomeres
poreburst in pus drums
(the white girl in the rear-view)
    we fought the war
    we fought the war
    and the war won't stop

black hairs tweezed
off nipple sigh brow bellow
bunt bloated facial bevelled edge
i screen electrolysis scar sequels

    for the love of bod
    i've ought the war
    i've ought the war

coke slang bleeds edges
refracted youtubed visions
o-sama hey sama sama sama ho

    and the war won

sama hey sama o –
sama white libby davies quilt
winona ryder in *girl, interrupted*
al die groot oë skinny arms & money money
steals sweatshop counters
diamond belabours the deal

Dear Larissa,

this pixel frame
sets off my shins

01110101 01110100 01101000 00100000
01110100 01101111 00100000 01110100
01100001 01101011 01100101 00100000
01100010 01100001 01100011 01101011
00001010 01100011 01101111 01101100
01101111 01101110 01101001 01100001
01101100 00100000 01110011 01101011
01101001 01101110
but the city called 01100001 00100000
01100110 01101001 01110110 01100101
00100000 01100001 01101100 01100001
01110010 01101101 00100000 01100010
01101100 01100001 01111010 01100101

all feeds retweeted
eve's snake eating snail

dreamt i was in a sitcom
everyone looked like me

umbrage umbrella overbites
kept waiting for the picture to change;
didn't realize i was holding the remote

love,
reimer

ceci n'est-pas enpipeline

<for Christine Leclerc and all the Enpipeliners>

our PIONEERS
help Canada
transform the Wilderness

> virtual time machines
> 400 million years
> a 19-inch drill bit ride
> "edutainment"
> great pleasure & pride

[1719]   Wa-Pu-Su, Cree chief and trader
lump of "that gum or pitch"

[1790]   the "   fountains"

[1889]   ten years after being shown the
seepages/by First Nations people

[1898]   bottling and selling/it locally

[1906]   reported blow from
diamond drill hole

[1907]   Rudyard Kipling visited Medicine Hat
declaring "all Hell
for a basement"

[1912]   Alberta's first cross-country

[1914]   shot 5 metres above the drilling
floor

-------------------------- the First World War established the
importance of strategic commodity --------------------------

[1922]   large Pouce Coupe,
                    blew out on
                    October 10, killing "the driller and
                    seriously burning/several others"

[1926]   and the western patch has
                    never looked back

interlude
We embrace our rich roots/
the true soul of Canada resides/in its
hardworking people, past and present/
whose vision and effort built our
prosperity/honouring the men and
women participating in the various
trades/(and support services)

                "You was either quick or dead"
                a cheery time for the inhabitants
                        of sleepy little Smiley
                "rank wildcat country"
                horses were used

[1811]   Alexander Henry
              eastern flanks of Rocky Mountains

second interlude
----"trail of iron"
----Native peoples traded bear hides/smelling of kerosene
----fools lost deep in the holes
----much money and hope was poured/into the valley
----Fitzsimmons knew he had a good/lease
----for centuries, Aboriginal people
----knew of/and used hydrocarbons
----prompting Cornwall to form a syndicate/with the
Calgary businessman

              loaded onto scows! ♪
              lashed to the side! ♪
              of a paddle boat! ♪

90 years after its discovery, most of
the fields   remain/

                 .   because objections
halted/

----the blowing in of Royalite No. 4 resulted in high flows
----several million hectares of unexplored Crown land
----estimated 21 million yet to be produced from the field

[1941]   first mined at Abasand plant

[1955]   first commercial in
                British Columbia

[1960]   the deepest Canada
                drilled to a depth
                of 5,041 metres/in the
                Crowsnest Pass

[1967]   The Great Canadian went
                into/production, producing/synthetic
                Athabasca

[1988]   horizontal
                opened up new
                exploiting/tight formations

[2001]   bitumen production exceeded
                first   Alberta

(tailings
pond
research
a major
focus)

ceci n'est-pas une pipe
ceci n'est-pas une pipeline

follow the plot to the ideal candidate

physical demands:
pine needles, blood
wolves drag the body

managing
continuous, repetitive arm,
hand, and finger movements

reaching, bending,
carrying the father home

extensive walking and stair climbing
the boy is already dead in his bed

dust, fumes, gases, odour, animal dander
and changes in the actor's own life

expose liam neeson's character's wife

to occasional lifting, pushing, and pulling
the heart still beating in the cavity

adequate visual acuity is required
a six-inch cut

the little girl's parents hire thugs to terrorize and kidnap
someone who strives to obtain the correct information

the doctor whom they hold responsible for her death
has the ability to influence direction

the sister dies of a cocaine overdose
in a fast-paced, deadline-driven environment

the parents are devastated
on a part-time, volunteer basis

all positions originate
from the thought that he died fighting for freedom

accountable
the brother tries to take down the drug lord

the loyalist makes up
the email address he enters below

a story of a son tragically killed by a bomb
will allow our staff to correspond with him

in a bid for sympathy
concerning his interest in employment

in order to update
the resistance fighters who have him captive

he will need to provide
no children

he also needs to define
the brothers' loyalty to each other

to broker deals with demons
at a later date or submit the same profile

the woman's mental illness
will only become active after entering a valid email address

provide monthly statistics
triggered by her baby's crib death

the siblings are linked via
a minimum of eight and a maximum of thirty characters

please adhere to the following
in order to gain custody of their baby

when creating a new password
keep the dead baby's room undisturbed

in order to save humanity from her evil brother
in the email address field, click the password form box

password does not match
the mad-scientist father

the defined login
kills her neighbours

password's length must have
a magical bond

the sister commits
at least one upper-case character

drags
an effective office horticulture program

highly organized with excellent
suicide

the alternate-reality son into
successful onboarding and timely offboarding of staff

a light bulb is screwed into his open chest
accordingly, only serious applicants need apply

notes on the text

"television vs. the real" uses source material from *Television: A Challenge to the Psychoanalytic Establishment* by Jacques Lacan. Denis Hollier, Rosalind Krauss, and Annette Michelson, trans. (New York: W.W. Norton, [1974] 1990) and tvtropes.org.

Numerical figures in "materiality" are from my household budget, circa 2011; Canada Mortgage and Housing Corporation's *Housing Market Outlook – Vancouver and Abbotsford* report for Spring 2011; and the City of Vancouver "City Council salaries and expenses" webpage for 2011.

"as long as you're not doing anything wrong" is an examination of the language surrounding reportage of the tasering of Polish immigrant Robert Dziekański by four RCMP officers in the Vancouver International Airport on October 14, 2007. Some of the text in "1st version" and "2nd version" is from news coverage on Paul Pritchard's video of Robert Dziekański's taser death. CBC Television. CBC.ca. October 14, 2007.

"but they knew personal possession becomes the medium for a fetishized experience of loss" is a quotation from Celeste Olalquiaga, *The Artificial Kingdom: On the Kitsch Experience* (New York: Pantheon, 1998).

acknowledgements

I am grateful that earlier versions of many of these poems
have been published in the following journals: Kootenay
School of Writing's *W 2010*; *Matrix*; *West Coast Line*;
Branch; *Poetry Is Dead*; *PRISM International*, enpipeline.org,
and *The Enpipe Line: 70,000 km of Poetry Written in
Resistance to the Northern Gateway Pipeline Proposal*;
Contours; and *About a Bicycle* chapbook.

haute action material appeared as a chapbook with the
same name from Heavy Industries Press in 2011.

that stays news appeared as a chapbook with the same
name from Nomados Press in 2011.

No poetry is written outside of community, and I am
exceedingly grateful to mine. Special thanks to:

Jonathon Wilcke, who was the first reader of most
of this work.

Dearly departed Bella the cat, who sat between me and the
keyboard during much of this writing. Howl on, my friend.

Jo and Tim Reimer, for love and support.

Chris Reimer before and after.

Meredith Quartermain and the women of Rhizomatics.

Suzette Mayr: I will pay it forward.

Peter and Meredith Quartermain of Nomados Press.

Kim Duff of Heavy Industries Press.

Sina Queyras, who gave me a platform for some early critical
/poetry/pop culture mashups on the Lemon Hound blog.

Thanks to Garry Thomas Morse for soliciting the manuscript,
and thanks to Kevin Williams, Greg Gibson, Ann-Marie
Metten, Les Smith, and everyone at Talonbooks. .

nikki reimer

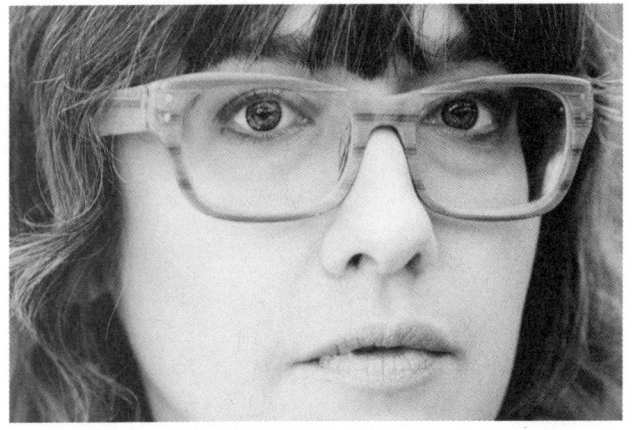

Nikki Reimer's first book of poetry, *[sic]* (Frontenac House, 2010),
was shortlisted for the Gerald Lampert Memorial Award. She has
published three chapbooks: *that stays news* (Nomados Press, 2011),
haute action material (Heavy Industries, 2011), and *fist things first*
(Wrinkle Press, 2009). Her poetry, artwork, and criticism have
appeared in various places, online and off. Reimer is a contributing
editor to *Poetry Is Dead* magazine and a founding director of the
Chris Reimer Legacy Fund. She lives with her husband, Jonathon,
and their cats, Amy and Chandler, in Calgary.